Face the Facts

Animal
Welfare

Bel Browning

For information, address the publisher:
Raintree, 100 N. LaSalle, Suite 1200, Chicago, IL 60602

Design by Mayer Media/Jane Hawkins
Printed and bound in China.

07 06 05 04 03
10 9 8 7 6 5 4 3 2 1

Library of Congress Cataloging-in-Publication Data

Browning, Bel.
  Animal welfare / Bel Browning.
    p. cm. -- (Face the facts)
Summary: Gives an overview of the treatment and care that animals receive from humans, the potential for abuse in such areas as farming and research, and the ethics and consequences of animal abuse.
Includes bibliographical references and index.
  ISBN 0-7398-6430-0
  1. Animal welfare--Juvenile literature. [1. Animals--Treatment.] I.
Title. II. Series.
  HV4708 .B77 2003
  364.1'87--dc21
                                2002012853

Acknowledgments
The publishers would like to thank the following for permission to reproduce photographs:
pp. 2–3, 6–7 MPM Images; p. 4 Ted Horowitz,/Corbis Stockmarket; p. 5 Mug Shots/Corbis Stockmarket; pp. 8–9 Paul A. Souders/Corbis; pp. 10–11 Private Collection/Bridgeman Art Library; pp. 12–13 Museum of the City of New York/Corbis; p. 14 Laurent Touzeau/Still Pictures; p. 15 Suzanne Plunkett/Associated Press; pp. 16–17 Heine Pedersen/Still Pictures; p. 18 Daniel Dancer/Still Pictures; p. 19 Aldo Brando/Still Pictures; p. 20 Roland Seitre/Still Pictures; p. 21 Gail Mooney/Corbis; p. 22 Detlef Konner/Still Pictures; p. 23 Klein/Hubert/Still Pictures; pp. 24–25 Lynne M. Stone/Nature Picture Library; p. 26 Thomas Raupach/Still Pictures; p. 27 Peter Dean/FLPA; p. 28 M & C Denis-Huot/Still Pictures; p. 29 Rex Harper/RSPCA Photolibrary; p. 30 Liz Cook/RSPCA Photolibrary; p. 31, 37 Ron Kirkby/RSPCA Photolibrary; p. 33 Keith Weller/Associated Press; p. 34 Jeremy Horner/Corbis; p. 35 Harmut Schwarzbach/Still Pictures; p. 38 Michel Gunther/Still Pictures; p. 39 Paul Vodden/RSPCA Photolibrary; pp. 40–41 Humane Society/Associated Press; p. 43 Minden Pictures/FLPA; pp. 44, 45 Reuters/Popperfoto; pp. 46–47 Alban Donohoe/RSPCA Photolibrary; p. 48 Kevin Fleming/Corbis; p. 49 Tom Stewart/Corbis Stockmarket; p. 51 J. J. Alcalay/Still Pictures.

Cover photograph: NHPA.

Some words are shown in bold, **like this.**
You can find out what they mean by
looking in the Glossary.

Contents

Introduction

Animal welfare is an everyday issue. It is also one that can provoke strong reactions. Influenced by science, economics, and ethics, it considers the treatment that animals receive from humans. The well-being of an animal is determined by factors such as health and whether or not it suffers. The study of animal welfare must ask questions like:

- What effects do human actions have on animals?
- Should people try to improve animals' lives, and how?
- How can people find out about pain and suffering in animals?

People share this planet with millions of other animal species. Humans are distinguished from these species by their complex societies, languages, and the technology they have created. Human intelligence and technology means we have more power than any other type of animal on earth.

At first this power was expressed through the hunting of other animals for food. Today animals are even more important to humans. People eat animals, use their skins for shoes and clothes, and keep them for work. Drugs and chemicals are also tested on them. They are used for sports such as horse and dog racing, and entertainment such as circuses. They are loved and cared for as pets, and sometimes used as religious symbols.

For centuries opinion has been divided over animals. At one extreme are the animal rights campaigners, who believe that we should not even keep pets, let alone experiment on or eat animals. At the other end of the scale are those who argue that animals are simply another resource for humans to use as they see fit (like coal or crops), and do not require any consideration.

Many people occupy a middle ground. They may keep pets, but be vegetarian. They may buy cruelty-free cosmetics (not tested on animals), but enjoy hunting. These points of view can change under certain conditions. If a person were starving, he or she would be more likely to eat meat that they would not normally touch.

Animal welfare has a long history but is in the news today more than ever before. On average a person eats 1,100 animals over a lifetime. Over 13 million unwanted pets are destroyed each year in the United States. The RSPCA (Royal Society for the Prevention of Cruelty to Animals) in Australia investigated 77,000 cruelty complaints in the year 2000. This book looks at why animal welfare issues are so important, and how they affect people today.

These boys watch a bear through the glass side of its tank at a zoo.

5

What Is Animal Welfare?

In 1948 many nations around the world agreed to the Universal Declaration of Human Rights. This document describes basic rights such as "the right to life, liberty, and security of person."

If humans deserve rights, do animals? Those who think animals do not have rights argue that humans are very different from other animals. Humans have the ability to reason, build machines, and use complex systems of communication. People's intellectual and cultural superiority, some argue, means they deserve different treatment from animals. Human illness, starvation, and suffering should be reduced, no matter what the consequences are for other animals.

Other people want animals to have rights, saying that they have many similar needs and feelings even if they are less intelligent. Those who support animal welfare believe that whether we give animals rights or not, we still have a responsibility to look after them.

What about welfare?

Welfare is the state of well-being in which basic needs are met and suffering is minimized. Animal welfare is concerned with the suffering of individual animals and ways to improve their well-being—not just the threat to a species. Humans can recognize issues affecting their own welfare. For example, you know if you're hungry or thirsty. However, it is harder for humans to judge an animal's welfare. Could you tell if a pig's grunt meant she was hungry, thirsty, or afraid?

In recent years it has been proven that animals have specific needs. If these needs are not met, their welfare may be compromised. In response to this information, the Farm Animal Welfare Council, an internationally recognized organization in Great Britain, developed the Five Freedoms as standards for farm animals:

- Freedom from hunger and thirst
- Freedom from discomfort
- Freedom from pain, injury, and disease
- Freedom from fear and distress
- Freedom to express normal behavior

These freedoms now form the basis of policies and standards for many animal welfare organizations. In addition animal freedoms are slowly finding their way into legislation around the world.

"It matters not to the animal how we feel but what we do."

(John Webster in *Animal Welfare*, published 1994)

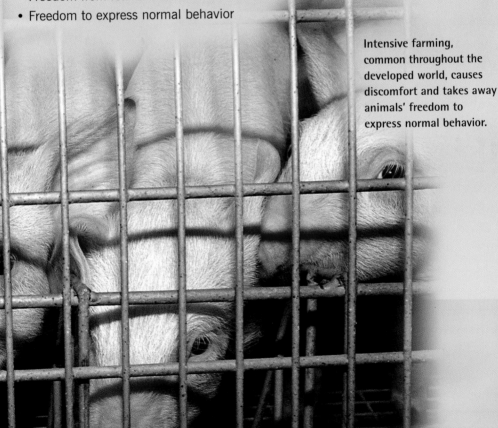

Intensive farming, common throughout the developed world, causes discomfort and takes away animals' freedom to express normal behavior.

Pain and Suffering

One of the problems with discussions about animal welfare is that the animals themselves cannot tell us how they feel. Instead people must study them to find out answers to questions such as: Do animals feel pain? Do animals suffer? Is suffering cruelty?

Physical pain

Physical pain is the body's way of protecting itself. When you touch something hot, you feel pain and move away. This limits the damage done. In order to feel pain, an organism needs a highly developed nervous system. Nerve endings detect sensations like pain or temperature and tell the brain. The brain's pain center dulls pain by causing the release of **hormone** painkillers such as **endorphins** and **cortisones.**

Mammals, fish, and birds all have pain control centers in their brains. All **vertebrate** animals produce pain-controlling substances like endorphins, too. In fact even earthworms have been found to make endorphins.

Being separated from the rest of the flock is highly stressful for sheep.

Mental and emotional pain

It may be easy to spot poor physical health, but we cannot read an animal's mind to find out what it is feeling. However, evidence does suggest that animals experience mental pain and stress. In one experiment researchers measured hormone levels in sheep while they were being loaded into a truck, put through a **sheep dip,** or chased by a dog. Levels of cortisone-type hormones, used as painkillers by the body, rose in all these situations. This indicates a high level of stress and pain in the experimental subjects. The worst affected were those sheep separated from the flock. It appears that to a sheep, a solo dip is much more stressful than being taken to the slaughterhouse with the rest of the flock.

Suffering and sentience

Pain causes suffering. Since we know that mammals, birds, and fish at least can feel pain, we might conclude that they suffer, too. The capacity to suffer by feeling pain, injury, and discomfort is described as **sentience.** Animals that are judged at present to be **nonsentient** include insects, spiders, and shellfish. New Zealand is one of the few places that recognizes crabs and lobsters as sentient and has laws to protect them. The sentience of an animal affects how we treat it in the law and in practice.

One danger of exploring animal needs is that we may fall into the trap of **anthropomorphism**—assuming animals think and feel as we do. The sheer number of cartoons with talking, thinking animals shows how common anthropomorphism is in our everyday lives. However, it is incorrect to assume that animals have needs or emotions that are similar to those of humans.

The History of Animals and People

The story of people on Earth is one of competition between humans and the rest of the animal kingdom. The first humans were hunter-gatherers. They collected seeds and fruits and caught animals for food and clothing. Cave paintings depict brutal and dangerous kills—as dangerous to people as to their prey.

About 7,000 years ago, people first began to practice agriculture. Tribes settled on plots of land where they grew crops and kept animals. These people began the slow process of **domesticating** and taming animals such as cattle.

Domestication offers the advantages of food and safety to animals. These animals had to be kept in conditions good enough to allow them to do their work or be slaughtered for food at the required time. Humans gained a guaranteed supply of working animals and food that could be harvested on demand.

Super animals

Once animals were under human control, people could start to improve their quality. Choosing to mate the best animals together, farmers could breed

even better offspring. Most domestic animals today are much larger than their wild relatives. They produce more milk, or are easier to herd, or give birth to more young. These "super animals" now need us as much as we need them. The Belgian Blue cow, for example, is bred to be "double muscled" for extra meat. It cannot give birth without human intervention. A Belgian Blue calf is usually born by **cesarean section** because it is too big for natural birth.

"Super animals" were bred and proudly displayed in the 1700s and 1800s. This Gloucester Old Spot pig (a type of pig bred to be very large) was painted in Great Britain.

Respect for Animals

Throughout history people have tamed and changed animals. However, they have also shown them great respect. Ancient Egyptians are known to have worshiped animal gods like the jackal Anubis. They are also known to have loved cats. In a cemetery near Cairo, 180,000 **embalmed** cats were recently discovered. Only rich people could afford embalming, so cats must have been prized. Hindus in India still consider cows to be holy, so they do not slaughter them.

Blood sport

In contrast to the Egyptians, ancient Romans mutilated and killed thousands of animals in lavish public festivals. When the Colosseum was opened, 5,000 animals were killed in just one day. Similar forms of entertainment continue to be popular throughout the world today in the form of bullfighting and rooster and dog fights.

At the same time, the Romans also built up strong relationships with other animals. Dogs were tamed for protection and to help with hunting. Donkeys and oxen were used for work; cows, goats, and sheep provided milk and meat; and horses were used for travel.

11

Seeds of change

As animals began to feature more prominently in the domestic lives of humans, so the relationship between the two started to change. Having more contact with tamed animals allowed people insight into animal behavior and instincts. For some, there might be profit to be made from this behavior—perhaps the retrieving skills of a dog. In others, experiences with a pet might mean they had a great deal of sympathy for animals.

Significant campaigns for animal welfare began just over 200 years ago. Before this time many religions hinted at some obligation to animals out of respect for the Creator, but many people saw animals as little more than machines. Early animal welfare campaigners came from the wealthier parts of society. The rich came into contact with animals through riding horses or having pets. They also had the time and influence to become involved in making animal welfare laws.

The struggle to create laws that protect animals has been going on for centuries. When **bull baiting** was banned in Great Britain in 1835, not everyone approved. Just years earlier in 1827, the prime minister, George Canning, had commented on bull baiting, saying that "the amusement inspired courage and produced a nobleness of sentiment and elevation of mind." Much of the general public agreed with Canning, since this sport offered entertainment in both town and country. These opinions were overridden by people who believed that animals were suffering and decided to act in their defense.

Science played some part in fostering sympathy for animals. Scientific research and observations led to a better understanding of animals. With the growth of newspapers and inexpensive books, more people became aware of animal issues.

Another factor was the advance of philosophy and human rights. The abolition of slavery in the United States and in the British Empire sparked consideration of animal rights, too. As philosophers and intellectuals began to write that some animals were **sentient,** campaigners began to spread the idea that animals deserved consideration.

As interest in animal welfare began to grow, laws were passed to protect animals. The first welfare society, the Society for the Prevention of Cruelty to Animals was formed in Britain in 1824. Known today as the Royal Society for the Prevention of Cruelty to Animals (RSPCA), it is the oldest animal protection organization in the world, and has been the inspiration for similar organizations around the world. The ASPCA (American Society for the Prevention of Cruelty to Animals) opened in 1866 and was the first of its kind in the United States.

This painting shows American country life for the wealthy in the 1800s, when animal welfare concerns began to grow.

Growth and Progress

In recent centuries the global human population has increased rapidly. In 1600 the world's population was an estimated 3.5 million people; today it has grown to roughly 6 billion. This population explosion has had an effect on humans and the lives they lead, as well as on animals.

A direct by-product of the population increase has been the loss of **habitat** for animals. In the developed countries of the world, a tremendous amount of land must be farmed to support these billions of people. Even more land must be developed for housing, roads, and industry. Where people have congregated in cities, the natural world has had to accommodate garbage dumps, exhaust fumes, and other pollution.

To afford to eat and have a good quality of life, people need jobs. Advancing technology has meant that the majority of new employment is industrial and city-based. Few people in cities are able to farm their own food, so with basic needs such as food at stake, **intensive farms** have become a necessity. Globally around 43.5 billion animals are farmed for food (such as meat and milk) each year.

This fox searches through garbage to find something to eat.

The result of this progress is that humans have an enormous impact on, and influence over, animals' lives. This has prompted some people to organize themselves into animal welfare groups. Today there are over 6,000 animal welfare organizations around the world.

Some have a general interest in all aspects of animal welfare, for example the ASPCA in the United States and RSPCA in Britain. In contrast, the Anti-Dog-Meat Movement has a specific goal: to end the breeding, sale, and slaughter of dogs for meat.

Origins of some of the first national animal protection organizations

Country	1st regional organization	National organization	Name of organization
United States	1866	1866	ASPCA
England	1824	1824	RSPCA
Scotland	1839	1990s	Scottish SPCA
Australia	1871	1981	RSPCA Australia
New Zealand	1882	1933	Royal New Zealand RSPCA
World	1953	1981	World Society for the Protection of Animals

A Global Viewpoint

Animal and human welfare are often in opposition. We need to feed and house billions of people, some of whom do not have enough to eat. Doing this while making sure that all animals live in ideal circumstances is impossible. Sometimes, however, a single global cause unites people from a wide variety of backgrounds to fight for animal welfare.

Whaling

In 1986 the International Whaling Commission placed a **moratorium** or ban on commercial whale hunting for food and scientific research. This was brought about by continued pressure from conservation and animal welfare organizations around the world.
Falling whale numbers and the inhumane

Iceland is one of the few countries that is in favor of whaling.

killing techniques used had shocked members of these organizations and the general public.

Most countries stuck to this ban, but 20,000 whales have been killed for food, cosmetics, and scientific reasons since the ban. Technology has made whale products such as oil and whalebone unnecessary, but they are still desirable as luxury goods. This fuels the continued harpooning of **endangered** whale species.

Elephant attack

A good instance of a clash between people and animals comes from India. Rapid population growth has forced farmers to convert more and more forest into agricultural land. This forest was the home of elephants, which have begun to raid farms and attack people. In July and August 2001, twenty elephants were deliberately poisoned in Sonitpur, near Nameri National Park. In September, eleven more elephants died a similar death. Local people trying to protect their crops from damage were almost certainly responsible.

Media watch

Daily papers love a good animal story because they are always popular, and papers with fascinating headlines sell themselves. In the summer of 2001, terrorists were planting bombs in Jerusalem, and the trials of suspects of the U.S. embassy bombings in Nairobi, Tanzania, and Kenya were under way. The media, however, chose to focus on an animal story. In Washington state a moose was spotted cooling off in a swimming pool. It made headline news around the world.

Wildlife

Wildlife and humans are often in opposition. Through activities such as logging, building, farming, and polluting, humans destroy animal **habitats** Most of the animals on our planet have become specialized to live in a particular habitat. If this disappears because of human activities, such as draining wetlands or cutting down forests, they cannot survive.

Killing animals for food and sport by hunting and **snaring** is common practice across the globe. In the United States, for example, hunters kill over 200 million animals each year. Some of these animals are killed for food, some are killed to control populations, and others are killed for recreation. Death is often quick and efficient—but not always. An animal that is injured in a hunt but gets away may take weeks to die. Snares are not selective at all and can trap or harm any animal that gets caught in them. Supporters of hunting with dogs argue that it offers the best way to control animal numbers, but the animal may be chased to exhaustion for many miles before capture and death.

The garbage (wrappers and bags and cans) that people discard can be deadly to wild animals. They may get trapped inside metal cans, or choke on plastic bags. In 1998 a dead whale was washed ashore on the Spanish coast. Its stomach contained a deadly meal of over 44 pounds (20 kilograms) of plastic bags and bottles.

A great deal of animals get killed on roads each year. In Florida thousands of animals from more than 80 species are

annually killed attempting to cross a two mile (three kilometer) stretch of road in Paynes Prairie State Park. To help prevent these deaths, an innovative group developed a concrete barrier that prevents most animals from crossing the road. Now the animals follow the barrier to one of several tunnels built under the road, where they can safely cross to the other side. "Frog crossings" such as this, and other structures built over and under roads, work very well.

Some animals, especially fish and **corals,** are often taken from the wild and left to die and dry out in the sun to be sold as souvenirs. The shells, starfish, and sea horses sold in vacation resorts are all harvested from the sea.

Conch shells are popular tourist souvenirs. Native people, such as this man in Colombia, can make money by harvesting them from the ocean and selling them.

This photo was taken in Oregon. Deforestation destroys the habitats of many species.

Zoo Life

Zoos and **aquariums** have existed for around 4,500 years. The first collections of animals were made by the rich and famous as a hobby, as a reflection of their success, and to gain scientific knowledge of behavior. Today zoos are run as businesses and the 10,000 zoos around the world house between 2 and 5 million animals.

Zoos are seen as important for the preservation of rare species, breeding rare animals for reintroduction into the wild. Zoos are also educational, offering people the chance to observe captive animal behavior—and this can often be entertaining. In addition, animals may have an easier life than they would in the wild, not having to hunt for food and shelter.

Zoos also face a lot of criticism. In 1994 a survey revealed that only 16 out of 145 reintroduction programs had been successful, suggesting that their conservation role needs to be improved. Zoos have a poor conservation record because in reality, not many of them have an active conservation role, preferring to keep species that are more common and easy to care for. Animals in captivity do not always behave in a natural way. They may resort to violence or self-mutilation to relieve boredom. These disturbed and sometimes dangerous animals may be **put down.**

Zoos arouse strong opinion on both sides. Even their supporters recognize that thousands of zoos, especially in poor or war-torn countries, cause animal suffering. But sometimes zoos have played a useful role in keeping an **endangered** species going, as well as educating people about animals.

In many existing zoos, conditions could be made better. Animal rights activists say this makes sense not just for the animals but for visitors too, who will see animals leading more normal and healthy lives, thus presenting a more authentic look at animal behavior.

Zoo improvements

Today many zoos are better recognizing the physical and mental needs of the animals under their care. In a barren enclosure, an animal will often resort to **stereotypies,** the repetition of movements like pacing or foot chewing, that continues even when blood is drawn.

Stereotypies are clear signs of frustration and stress. The animal is trying to calm itself through repeated behavior. Improving an animal's environment can help stop stereotypies.

These examples have all worked well:

- Austin Zoo in Texas hides capuchin monkey treats inside Chinese take-out boxes. The challenge of finding the treats allows the monkeys to use their natural skills and reduces their levels of boredom.

- Glasgow Zoo reduced pacing among ocelots by increasing feeding from one to four times a day. Keepers hide chopped meat in a woodpile so the cats spend the day hunting for their food.

- At Copenhagen Zoo the bears are kept busy and happy with a honey machine. Honey is pumped into artificial trees at random times of the day. Hearing this, the bears climb the trees and begin the sticky job of collecting the honey.

Farm Animals

In the developed world, farmers are usually the only people who live alongside the animals they farm and eat. Many consumers eat and wear animal products with little idea of how the animals lived. Many people still imagine farms to be places with cattle in fields, pigs in pens, and chickens scratching in the dirt. The reality can be very different.

High-tech farms

Intensive farming systems do not resemble traditional farms at all. From the outside these modern farms are sterile rows of long, low buildings. The only signs of life are the trucks that pull in to load up the animals ready for slaughter or to deliver feed. The cleaning and feeding is all mechanized at intensive farms.

These "factory" farms have their roots in the last century. Farming had to become more efficient and occupy less space to supply the expanding cities' demand for fast and cheap food. The United States increased production levels after World War I when surplus food could be sold at a profit to a hungry Europe. After World War II, Europeans were tired of food rationing. They wanted meat, and plenty of it. Helped by government funding, the intensive farm was born. Once medicines were created to stop diseases from spreading in the cramped conditions, they became a huge success.

Farm animals are kept in cages or pens in barns—or even high-rise buildings with slatted floors that allow waste to drop through. It is easier to feed, water, and give medicine to the animals when they are housed indoors. Light levels are constant—either low (to discourage fighting), or high (to encourage hens to lay eggs).

For transportation to the slaughterhouse, animals are usually crowded together. Those that fall may be injured or crushed. The open, slatted trucks give little protection against heat or cold—a shock for animals from temperature- and light-controlled environments. Many countries have regulations requiring rest and feeding stops, but these are not always obeyed. On long journeys mortality rates can be high. For example, more than 100,000 Australian sheep die each year on the trip to the Middle East, where demand for lamb is high.

Once they reach the slaughterhouse, cows, sheep, and pigs are stunned using an electric shock, or **captive bolt,** to the brain. Occasionally this does not work, so some animals are still conscious when they are killed. Cows and pigs are usually killed by having their throats slit.

Animals have been shown to suffer in some of the very conditions that ensure efficient and cheap production. Modern chickens bred for speedy growth are ready to be eaten at 41 days old. Such speedy growth means intensive animals often have heart and leg defects that can cripple or kill them. However, these chickens, like other intensively farmed animals, meet consumer desire for cheap and readily available meat.

"These intensively raised animals have no constitution, you know. Sometimes they just seem to get heart failure because of the strain imposed by terrific growth rates. And often their legs or backs seem to give out: they grow so fast that their bone structure cannot keep up."

(Chris Turton, chicken farmer, Great Britain)

Free-Range Farms

Toward the end of the 20th century, people began to take a greater interest in how their food was produced. Today we can choose to eat meat and other produce from animals raised on **nonintensive** and **free-range** farms.

Intensive egg production

In many factory farms, laying hens are housed five to a cage, with 69 square inches (450 square centimeters) of space for each bird. Sheds may hold up to 60,000 birds, whose eggs are collected from the cages by conveyor belt. This is a very economic egg production system, but it does have some problems. Hens frequently fight with their cage-mates and pluck out their own feathers to relieve stress. Lack of exercise means brittle bones are common and many die at an early age. Traditional breeds of hen, like their jungle-dwelling ancestors, can be aggressive, so new breeds have been developed with a calmer temperament. Various alternatives to factory farms have developed over the last twenty years.

Perchery systems
Percheries are large barns where hens have bare floor areas with an upper limit of about 25 birds per 10 square feet (1 square meter). In addition each bird has at least 2.5 square inches (15 square centimeters) of perching space.

Deep litter systems
Deep litter birds are also confined to the barn. There is usually a maximum of 7 birds per 10 square feet (1 square meter), and a third of the barn floor is covered with litter (bedding). The litter allows the birds to scratch around for food and carry bedding to their nests. Another addition is the presence of an area specifically designed for the collection of droppings.

Semi-intensive and free-range systems
Hens have some access to an outside area. (The amount of time spent outside can vary from farm to farm.) On the inside the barn has the same

conditions as perchery or deep litter systems. The outside compound typically offers enough room and the proper conditions for the birds to scratch and dust bathe freely. Based on the term, "free-range," many people assume that free-range farms give chickens continuous access to the outside during the day. However, since the legal definition of "free-range" is vague in the United States, eggs and meat labeled as such may actually be from semi-intensive farms. Some European countries have much stricter standards for what constitutes "free-range."

For the producer and consumer, intensively farmed hens produce the cheapest eggs. The labor, land, and food costs of mass production are lower, and this is passed on to the consumer. Barn systems offer more space per hen than intensive farms, and free-range even more. Since active hens eat more, land is expensive, and more people are needed to care for the birds, the cost to the farmer is higher. This cost is reflected in the price at the store. Free-range eggs and meat are more expensive for the shopper.

The Pig

After 12,000 years of **domestication**, pigs still have some traits of wild boars. Intelligent and inquisitive animals, they still root with their snouts for food (bulbs, worms, fruit, seeds, and leaves). Life on many farms, especially **intensive farms,** offers pigs no chance to do this.

Factory farm pigs

Breeding **sows** are confined in small stalls while they produce piglets for meat. One popular sow system is the stall or tether systems—now banned in some countries. The crate keeps the sow from turning around or taking more than two steps in any direction during her four-month pregnancy. Originally these stalls were designed to keep sows from fighting and make feeding and cleaning easier.

Before farrowing (giving birth) many sows are loaded into farrowing crates. Smaller even than a stall or tether, the sow may only stand up or lie down. She can only move slowly so her piglets have time to escape into the creep (a separate penned area) as she lies down. Once she is down, they can come back through the bars between the creep and the pen and suckle.

Intensively farmed pigs suffer from overcrowding and unnatural conditions.

A sow will have about ten to twelve piglets. At three weeks the piglets are taken for fattening. For the first six weeks, this may be in a metal pen. Then they go to the fattening house, often in bare pens with no bedding. Here they are kept in near darkness with up to 30 other piglets in the pen.

Profitable pigs

One of the useful things about this system is the quick turnaround of animals. The pigs grow much more quickly and can be sent to slaughter sooner than if they were raised in a more natural environment. The pigs are also much cheaper to rear using factory methods. Raising the temperature in the shed makes the pigs need less food. Antibiotics in the food prevent illness. All this also requires much fewer people to manage the process.

Intensive farms have drawbacks. A pregnant sow in the wild builds a large nest for her babies. In a factory farm, she becomes agitated and frustrated. Naturally, piglets drink milk up to about three months old. **Weaned** at three weeks on the farm, they suffer from the sudden change in food and the lack of warmth. They are also more likely to fight with other piglets.

Pig fighting, like zoo **stereotypies,** can be stopped. The addition of simple toys like a ball or bale of straw can greatly reduce behavior such as tail biting. But where economic interest is the driving force, this extra cost may not be a consideration since it would have to be passed on to the consumer. Where more animal-friendly systems have been introduced in pig farming, meat prices are considerably higher.

Pigs living in a free-range system have a more natural lifestyle. They have at least some outdoor access, and can move around, bathe, and root as in the wild.

Companion Animals

People keep **domestic** animals for companionship as well as for food. Pets are not bred for meat or milk, but for obedience and friendliness. They are not needed for food, but are kept as a luxury.

Pet life

In the wild most **sentient** animals grow up in a family. Peers and parents teach skills such as hunting. Adults are usually independent and may view others as competition for food, a companion, or a mate.

The lifestyle of a pet-store pet is totally different. In its most extreme form, pets such as puppies are reared by the hundreds in **intensive**-style farms. On these factory farms, puppies are cheap to produce and **weaned** for sale before eight weeks. The mother gets pregnant again right away.

A pet may have little contact with others of its species, and it may never be allowed to mate or breed. This is a very unnatural life, although that in itself may not be a problem. The crucial question is: can an animal adapt to these circumstances without suffering?

Causes of suffering

We do not know if animals "enjoy" their everyday lives as pets, but they often

This family of wild dogs in Tanzania have the freedom of a natural life, but are exposed to the dangers of the wild.

seem happy. Most pet owners love and care for their pets, giving them toys, food, and exercise. Unfortunately, there are also pet owners who are cruel to their pets. Cruelty can be caused by ignorance (lack of knowledge), neglect (lack of care), or outright cruelty (suffering caused by actively inflicted pain).

Animals that are unwanted or abandoned often end up at shelters. Although some find new homes, many have to be killed. The United States alone destroys 13 million pets a year. A shelter worker describes the difficulty of this situation, "There's a terrible paradox in what you have to do—you want to care for the animals, but you know you will have to kill some of them."

> **❝Animals are such agreeable friends—they ask no questions, they pass no criticisms.❞**
>
> (George Eliot, author [1819–1880])

> **❝Many pet animals enjoy a . . . higher standard of physical welfare than many children and . . . some horses retire into better care than that afforded to some old people.❞**
>
> (James Dewar, *The Rape of Noah's Ark*, 1969)

Many greyhounds are neglected after their racing life is over.

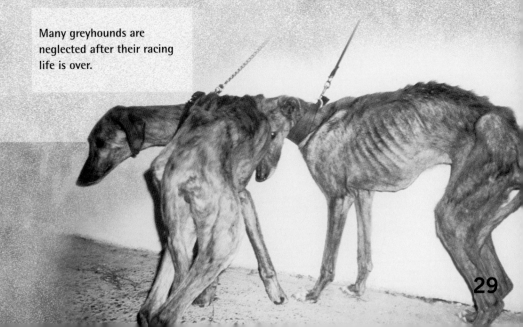

29

Research Animals

Animals have been used in scientific investigations for centuries. In the 1600s William Harvey studied the circulation of blood by performing experiments on both people and animals. In the 1800s Louis Pasteur found how to prevent chicken **cholera** through experiments infecting chickens with cholera bacteria. Since this time we have learned valuable scientific information from animal experimentation (sometimes known as **vivisection**) and continue to learn from over 100 million animals used around the world each year.

Why vivisection?

Vivisection has many purposes. Many countries have laws that require new chemicals to be safety-tested on animals before humans can use them. This testing includes new medicines, cosmetics, and toiletries that are tested internally and on the skin. Pioneering new surgical techniques, new vehicles, and sometimes even weapons are tested with animals standing in for people. Other research may simply be biological explorations of how the body works.

Learning from animal experiments can bring new possibilities for people, too. Animal **cloning** technology may someday lead to work on humans. Monkeys are in high demand for AIDS research because they are so similar to humans. In terms of science and medicine, humans can learn a lot from vivisection.

Beagles are used for research into the effects of smoking.

What are the alternatives?

Animal experimentation is only one of many techniques used to gain scientific knowledge. There are now several alternatives available.

Humans are the most reliable experimental subjects. For decades beagles have been forced to chain smoke so that scientists could investigate how smoking might affect people. More recently the large number of human smokers has been recognized as an equally valuable source of information, but animal tests continue.

Another way to study the effect of drugs and vaccines is through the use of human tissue. Only a small sample of tissue is needed, because it can be grown in a dish and used for testing. Microbes such as yeast and bacteria share similar cell structure and even some **DNA** with humans, so these can also yield realistic drug and vaccine test results. As technology improves, better test results and improved testing methods follow. Computer programs such as Cybermouse, which models how a real mouse would respond to tests, can be used in research. Realistic dummies can replace animals in crash tests for vehicles and weapons tests.

In many countries scientific research is tightly controlled and monitored by the government. Most experiments must be approved by specially selected panels.

Laboratory rats are bred for experimentation.

Genetic Engineering

Genetic engineering is a technique that is used to manipulate **genes** to produce animals that have enhanced qualities such as better milk production. It is distantly related to **selective breeding,** which has been used for centuries to give us the variety of pet and farm animals existing today. Many hundreds of thousands of animals are used every year in different countries for genetic engineering experiments.

New and improved

DNA can be found in every living cell of an animal or plant. This DNA contains all the information the organism needs to build and maintain the body. A length of the DNA that controls a specific characteristic— such as eye color—is called a gene.

Genetic engineering aims to change the genetic makeup of an organism by altering or moving its existing genes. Animals that have been altered in this way are called **transgenic** animals. Currently, in the early stages of this technology, around 100 animals are involved in the production of every three successful transgenic animals.

Genetic engineering has many benefits for humans. Through it we can discover:
- What specific genes do
- How to increase production of meat and milk
- Ways to create disease resistance
- Ways to create animals with diseases, for drug tests
- How to alter animals so we can use them as organ donors

However, in many cases there are some drawbacks. Animals may suffer from the experiments and from the conditions they live in. Many tests require sterile conditions, and to meet these, animals are separated at birth and live in cages without bedding or company. Animals are bred with deformities and must live under observation. Some are unable to move or see. Dolly the Sheep, famous for being a **cloned** copy of another adult sheep, has developed a painful form of arthritis at a surprisingly early age. Despite the pain she is in, Dolly will not be treated because scientists can learn from her sudden disability.

❝The alleviation of human suffering justifies the sacrifice of lower animals.❞

(Robert J. White, in *A Defense of Vivisection,*1976)

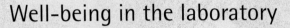

Well-being in the laboratory

Many laboratory animals experience pain and suffering, not just from the experiments, but also from the housing conditions. Many are kept in tiny cages with no companions. In the last few years, some researchers have begun to change the environments of these animals for the better. For example, a type of mouse engineered to have **neurological** problems has trouble walking. This disability allows scientists to study similar human diseases. The mouse, however, gets cold and hungry because it cannot make a nest or reach the food dispenser. After intervention by a welfare organization, the laboratory technicians put the food nearer to the mouse and added healthy mice that built a nest for all of them.

A genetically altered mouse is pictured next to a normal mouse. Researchers have genetically engineered mice to grow huge muscles. This may lead to the development of treatments for muscular dystrophy and other muscle-related disorders.

Opinions on Animal Welfare

Opinions are divided when it comes to animal welfare. Some people believe humans have priority over animals, due to their superior intelligence and ability. To others all life forms should have equal status and rights. Some issues, such as hunting or experimentation, inspire extreme views both for and against. There is no simple right or wrong answer, but there are many perspectives.

Religious viewpoints

Different religious writings portray animals in different ways. In the Judeo-Christian tradition, humans have the upper hand:

"Then God said 'Let us make man in our image, after our likeness and let them have dominion over the fish of the sea and over the birds of the air, and over the cattle, and over all the earth and over every creeping thing that creeps on the earth.'"

(The Bible)

Hinduism has a very different approach to the natural world:

"One should treat animals such as deer, camels, asses, monkeys, mice, snakes, birds, and flies exactly like one's own son. How little difference there is between children and these innocent animals."

(Srimad Bhagavatam)

Hindus honor the cow as the symbol of creation, Mother Earth. White cows wander freely in India.

In Islam the following opinion is expressed:

> "Doing good to beasts is like the doing of good to human beings, a deed of charity; while cruelty to animals is forbidden, just like cruelty to human beings."
>
> (Mishkat al Masabih)

Welfare and rights

Animal welfarists accept that humans have a big impact on animals' lives. They believe that humans have a responsibility for the well-being of animals—to avoid making them suffer. If this cannot be done, they believe that the suffering should at least be minimized.

Other animal rights supporters go further than the welfarists. They believe that animals have the right to be treated with respect and without **exploitation.** This means that animals should not be used for for farming, sports, or research. While some work peacefully through education and campaigning, others use violent ways to get their message across, such as sending letter bombs.

At the other end of the spectrum, many people support human rights over the rights of animals. These campaigners tend to join forces over specific issues. Many of the 20 million people who watch bullfights every year consider it to be an important cultural tradition as well as a sport. Hunters argue that animal numbers need to be controlled, or else the animals will starve during the winter. And a great many people simply believe that human life is more valuable, and so it is all right to use animals in medical experiments or for food.

Economics of Animal Welfare

Conditions or provisions that improve welfare often come at a high price. Farming is an excellent example of the relationship between animal welfare and economics. **Intensive farming** is the ideal way to produce animals cheaply and profitably. Many animals can be raised on a small area of land, and food and labor costs are lower than on extensive farms. The profit per animal is small, since supermarkets pay less for intensively reared meat, but the vast number of animals that can be produced compensates for this. In dairy farms for example, herd sizes and milk production in some countries have more than doubled since 1975. Although these mass production systems are efficient and economical, the well-being of the animals may be compromised.

Free-range farming usually offers higher levels of animal welfare, but also costs more because it requires larger land areas, more food, and more staff. To the public, free-range foods represent higher quality and so the products command a higher price. Stores pay the farmer more, and pass this price on to the consumer. With this premium price, a successful free-range farmer can in theory make a similar profit to an intensive farmer with fewer animals.

Many farmers are sympathetic to the well-being of their stock, but the expense of converting to a profitable free-range farm can be prohibitive. Productive land is an expensive commodity in the industrialized world. Other major expenses include the demolition of the intensive buildings and construction of new barns. The total cost of switching over, along with the fact that the farmer will not make much money while the conversion is taking place, can make it a very difficult switch to make. However, many Western governments, especially in northern Europe, are encouraging farmers to convert to organic methods (those with

a high regard for environmental and animal welfare concerns).

This pattern of animal welfare coming at a cost is a common one. Pet animals can also be very expensive to care for. The cost of providing a good standard of living for a pet dog throughout its life can cost up to $15,000 in the United States. A person interested in getting a pet has to decide if they can afford to provide the living conditions and attention the animal needs.

In the laboratory, not only are improvements to animal welfare expensive, but they may render some experiments impossible. Some experiments demand that animals be kept totally sterile, so even the introduction of a toy or bedding is impossible. If making such improvements in the animals' lives became law, these experiments could not continue.

Developing countries

Developing countries face different animal welfare problems. These countries also rely on agriculture, both for local use from small-scale producers, or as cash crops grown in bulk for the international market. Animals also play a part in other aspects of the economy. In some countries wild animals may be caught for sale as food, for the pet trade, or to research laboratories. Other animals such as bears are trained to dance, while baby animals can attract tourists who pay to see them.

In the developing world, famine, drought, and starvation are common. Countries struggle to support rapidly growing human populations and there are few, if any, animal protection laws. Many animals are being hunted to near extinction so that people may survive.

All available productive land is required to feed growing populations. Where land is poor, interest is growing in **intensive farms.** These farms are expensive to set up, however, and so the majority of farms are still run in a traditional way, with animals herded or tethered.

These animals from the Congo, a wild monkey and antelopes, will be sold for food.

Tortoise trading

Tortoises are one of the most popular animals in the exotic pet trade. More than 25 species are legally protected, and yet illegal trade continues to increase. A 2001 undercover investigation revealed rare tortoises openly for sale at markets in Morocco. Tortoise sellers assured the investigators that these animals could be imported to another country in a box or bag and were easy to care for.

In developing countries where the economy may be unsteady, animal trade is one of only a few sources of income. Animals like the tortoise are easily caught and packed up. In one illegal shipment opened by Dutch customs officials, 800 tortoises were packed in layers in a box. 50 were dead and 400 more were in a critical condition.

A large number had broken shells and missing legs. Had this cargo not been discovered and confiscated, the animals would have raised a substantial profit.

In recent years developing countries have benefited economically from the strict animal welfare regulations in developed countries. When cosmetic testing on animals is banned in one country, laboratories simply move elsewhere. This is often to the developing countries where the land and workforce is cheap, and new industries are vitally needed.

Animal Welfare Laws

Countries vary in the level of protection they offer to animals. This reflects their economic climates as much as the value placed on animals. A wealthy country can afford higher standards of living for animals. In countries facing famine and human suffering, animal welfare may not be such a priority. Examples of animal protection laws are given below.

United States

The U.S. Department of Agriculture (USDA) is the federal agency charged with enforcing the Animal Welfare Act (AWA). Congress originally passed the AWA in 1966 and has strengthened the language of the law four times since. The AWA provides protection for warm-blooded animals (other than farm or laboratory animals) from animal cruelty by providing minimum standards of care and treatment. On top of that, each state has its own animal protection laws. In 33 states animal abuse is classified as a felony instead of a misdemeanor.

Great Britain

The Protection of Animals Act of 1911 still operates and is much improved since its early days. The basic principles of the Act are that it is against the law and cruel to overload, beat, kick, mistreat, torture, or terrify an animal; to make an animal suffer when it does not have to; and to abandon an animal if it will suffer when it does not have to.

These puppies in Indiana have been packed into cages. The American Kennel Club is lobbying against legislation that would specify conditions for dog breeding.

New Zealand

It is considered an offense to knowingly cause an animal to become disabled, die, or have to be destroyed due to poor treatment. A person can be imprisoned for up to three years or fined $50,000.

European Law

Different countries throughout Europe have individual animal protection laws. Increasingly, however, the European Parliament is demanding that laws become standardized across the European Union.

Increased concerns over animal welfare are continually being reflected in new laws. For example, in 2001 the Humane Methods of Slaughter Act was passed by the U.S. Senate. Although existing acts from 1958 and 1978 were in place, these were not consistently upheld. This new act states that all animals must be made unable to feel pain before death, and that the Department of Agriculture must track any violations that occur.

International Cooperation

The Convention on International Trade in **Endangered** Species of Wild Flora and Fauna (CITES) recommendations to control the endangered species trade came into effect in 1975. To date, 146 nations including the United States and Great Britain have signed this agreement. The main purpose of the agreement is to prevent animals from becoming extinct, but it can affect individual welfare, too.

The countries in agreement with CITES prohibit commercial trade in endangered species. Now the animal trade has turned to smuggling to meet the demand for rare animals. The trade is second only to drug smuggling in its illegal moneymaking potential, with estimated revenues of $6 billion a year.

Despite CITES, animal smuggling is hard to control since exotic and rare species are highly desirable. People can often earn much-needed money from the capture and sale of creatures they have traditionally hunted for food and skins. Sometimes countries argue that the animals will be used for valuable research or breeding. However, many of the animals will suffer enormously during this process. About 75 percent of captured wild animals die in transit. Nine out of ten survivors will die in the following four years.

This trade is hard to detect and control. Some countries invest more than others in trying to prevent illegal trade. In Australia, for example, wildlife trade law is the most advanced in the world. The Wildlife Protection **Bill** of 2001 set the standard for the world, making it easier for the Australian government to **prosecute** offenders.

The world's most wanted bird

The deep-brilliant-blue Lear's macaw comes from northeast Brazil. Up until 1978 these birds were thought to be extinct. Only 98 Lear's macaws are known to exist. As a result they are the most wanted birds in the world, worth $125,000 each.

In 1988 three Lear's macaws were found in a house in Yorkshire, England. They had been smuggled into the country, perhaps inside other cargo. Mailing tubes are often used in smuggling. A bird is crammed headfirst into each end of the tube. Before they even arrive, most of them will be dead. Parrots often peck each other or themselves to death on their journey.

Hyacinth macaws are also endangered. These social birds travel in flocks or pairs. It is very stressful for them to be separated.

Campaigning for Change

Around the world animal laws show a great deal of variation. Laws are constantly being amended and updated, usually to introduce higher levels of protection for animals.

Many organizations involved in areas of the animal industry draw up their own codes of practice to ensure good standards. Frequently these codes become incorporated into law itself. Animal welfare organizations often research what is best for the animals and will attempt to get this recognized in **legislation.**

Changes to animal welfare legislation ßcome about when an issue is brought to the attention of the public and the government. Many governments have advisory bodies to oversee areas of potential concern. In the United States, animal welfare legislation (at the federal level) is heard in the House of Representatives committee on Agriculture and/or Resources. In the Senate, legislation goes before the Committee on Agriculture, Nutrition, and Forestry or the Environment and Public Works Committee. Animal welfare organizations that are not connected to the government, such as charities, may also be called on for their expertise.

Both multinational organizations that use animals and pressure groups from animal welfare organizations will lobby governments to support their interests.

Activists demonstrating against a bullfight in Montreal, Canada, 1999.

Companies with enough money to advertise the ways they have used animals for human benefit put forward a strong argument. Animal welfare organizations, who rely on public support and donations, have to be increasingly sophisticated and scientific if they are to make their case. The group that has the most effective campaign makes its point of view the most popular.

The process of lobbying includes researching and preparing evidence, statistics, and reports. The more the media is involved, the greater the chance of gaining the attention of the government. If the campaign is successful, new laws might be formed or old ones amended and reformed.

Before most elected officials will introduce animal-friendly legislation, they must be sure that there is sufficient public support. When the state of Virginia was

considering putting a bounty on coyotes, the governor received so much mail against the idea that he dropped the **bill.** The former governor of New York, Mario Cuomo, twice rejected a bill that would have allowed medical technicians to practice fitting human breathing tubes on cats. The Governor's office received more mail about this than any other piece of legislation.

Animal rights activists dressed as chickens protest against battery cages outside a meeting of European Union farm ministers in Brussels, 1999.

Animal Welfare and You

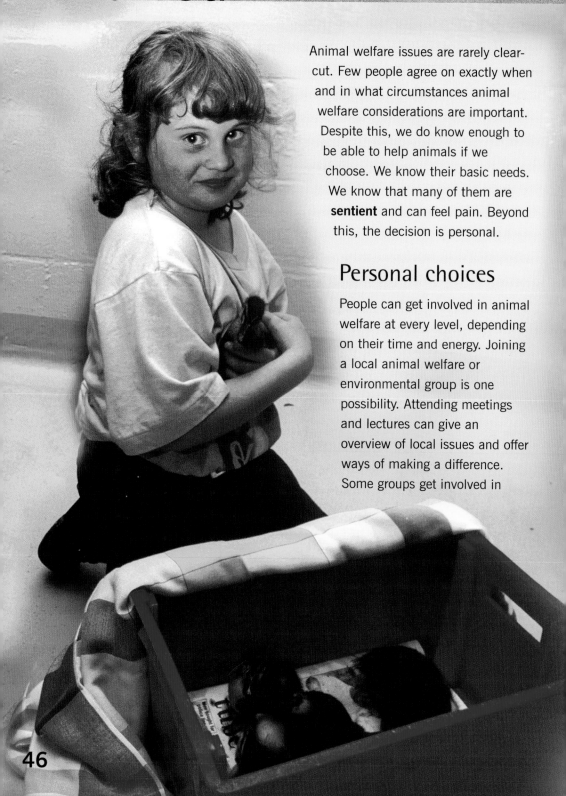

Animal welfare issues are rarely clear-cut. Few people agree on exactly when and in what circumstances animal welfare considerations are important. Despite this, we do know enough to be able to help animals if we choose. We know their basic needs. We know that many of them are **sentient** and can feel pain. Beyond this, the decision is personal.

Personal choices

People can get involved in animal welfare at every level, depending on their time and energy. Joining a local animal welfare or environmental group is one possibility. Attending meetings and lectures can give an overview of local issues and offer ways of making a difference. Some groups get involved in writing letters to government officials in order to raise awareness, giving you the chance to have a say in national politics.

Many animal shelters and clinics welcome volunteers, as their own funds may be limited. Volunteers may walk dogs or clean pens, helping to improve animals' lives and gaining valuable work experience at the same time.

Actions that we take in our everyday lives can directly influence animal welfare. The following suggestions are things you can do to help.

- If you see an act of cruelty, contact the police or the ASPCA or equivalent. Do not try to intervene—think of your own welfare first.

- If you have a pet, make sure you know how to care for it properly.

- Buy cruelty-free products when possible. If that is not an option, avoid "new" products, such as a new detergent, because they will have been developed with many more animal tests. Eco-friendly products are less polluting, which is beneficial to the health and welfare of animals and the environment.

- Disposing of garbage carefully can prevent accidental injury to wild animals.

- Shopping for **free-range** products promotes **nonintensive farming** and its associated standards of animal welfare. Going a step further would be to cut back on meat or become a vegetarian. The less meat is consumed overall, the less intensive production is needed to satisfy demand.

- Avoid using garden chemicals. Instead, encourage predatory wildlife such as ladybugs and birds to control unwanted insects. If you put up a house, bath, and feeder for birds, plant wild flowers, and recycle your organic waste in a compost heap, your garden will be well on the way to being animal friendly.

47

What Next?

Issues surrounding animal welfare can be complex. Research continually teaches us more, but there are still no easy answers. When human and animal interests are in competition, people support a wide range of opinions, according to their experience, knowledge, religion, and situation.

When people buy food, medicine, and clothes, they are involved in the animal debate. Consumers can often choose products that are more (or less) animal friendly. If they can afford to, they have the choice of buying **free-range** rather than **intensively farmed** meat. They can decide whether to wear fur or not. Leisure time can be spent fishing and hunting or swimming and hiking.

At the zoo, debate centers on keeping animals in captivity. There is proof that animals suffer in many zoos, but conditions can be improved. Zoos also play a role in the breeding and reintroduction of **endangered** species that would otherwise be lost.

Around the world there are billions of pets. Some of these have been caught illegally in the wild and transported to pet shops thousands of miles away. Puppies can be raised on huge puppy farms, or they can come from small litters and from breeders who care for their dogs.

> **"When I carefully consider**
>   **the curious habits**
>   **of dogs**
> **I am compelled to**
>   **conclude**
> **That man is the**
>   **superior animal.**
>
> **When I consider the**
>   **curious habits**
>   **of man**
> **I confess, my friend,**
>   **I am puzzled."**
>
> (Ezra Pound, poet [1885–1972])

The debate over animals used for scientific research is heated. Many researchers rely on animals as models for people. Animals are used in tests for cosmetics, weapons, and new treatments for deadly diseases such as AIDS and cancer. There is opposition to this research and the suffering it causes to animals, and so work continues to find suitable alternatives.

Animal welfare is a personal issue. People choose how to lead their lives, and directly and indirectly these choices can have an impact on animal welfare.

Facts and Figures

These are just a few of the things that are going on in the world where animals are involved.

Farming

Around 100,000 horses a year are involved in the production of **Hormone Replacement Therapies.** Pregnant mares are kept in small stalls for six months so that their urine can be collected. After birth the mare's foal is usually destroyed so that she can quickly get pregnant again.

The average person in the United States consumes about 215 pounds (98 kilograms) of meat every year.

In 1996, 760 million chickens were raised for meat in Great Britain. Of these, more than 45 million died early from illness and genetic defects.

Australia exports 5 million sheep to the Middle East each year.

Research

In addition to commercial animal tests, around $200 million a year is spent by the U.S. Department of Defense on animal research. This involves around 1.6 million animals. Examples of the research programs include shooting 700 cats to model human injuries, developing surgical techniques on pigs; and testing poison gases on rats and mice. Statistics in Britain for 2000 show that 2.71 million experimental procedures were carried out on animals. 500,000 of these animals were **genetically modified** (a 14 percent increase from 1999). In Australia 3 million animals were used in scientific research in 1998.

Companion animals

People often abandon pets, and in the United States 13 million unwanted pets are destroyed each year. The RSPCA in Britain rescued a badly neglected Monitor lizard from a house whose owner had moved. The lizard had an infection so severe it could no longer move, and was **put down** to end its suffering. In the year 2000, the RSPCA in Australia reported 47,000 cruelty investigations.

People also sometimes neglect to have their pets spayed or neutered, and if the pets escape the home they can breed, producing more unwanted animals.

Wildlife

The killer whale (orca) was first taken into captivity in 1961. Since then 134 others have been put in **aquariums.** In the wild they live over 50 years and swim more than 90 miles (150 kilometers) a day. In captivity 78 percent have died so far. Most have been less than six years old at death.

In the United States, at least 200 million animals are hunted each year; 3.5 million are trapped for fur.

In China and Korea, 7,500 bears are kept caged. Their bile is collected for medicine.

A killer whale performs in Aqualand, California.

51

Further Information

Contacts

American Anti-Vivisection Society
801 Old York Rd. #204
Jenkintown, PA 19046-1685
(215) 887-0816
e-mail: aavsonline@aol.com
www.aavs.org

American Welfare Institute
PO Box 3650
Washington, D.C. 20027
(202) 337-2332
www.awionline.org

ASPCA
424 E. 92nd Street
New York, NY 10128
(212) 876-7700
www.aspca.org

American Humane Association
63 Inverness Drive East
Englewood, CO 80112-5117
(800) 227-4645
e-mail: info@americanhumane.org
www.americanhumane.org

Americans for Medical Progress
908 King Street, Suite 301
Alexandria, VA 22314
(703) 836-9595
e-mail: info@amprogress.org
www.ampef.org

Foundation for Biomedical Research
818 Connecticut Avenue NW
Suite 200, Washington, D.C. 20006
(202) 457-0654
e-mail: info@nabr.org
www.fbresearch.org

Humane Society of the United States
2100 L Street NW
Washington, D.C. 20037
202-452-1100
e-mail: webmaster@hsus.org
www.hsus.org

International Fund for Animal Welfare
411 Main Street
PO Box 193
Yarmouth Port, MA 02675
(508) 744-2000
e-mail: info@ifaw.org
www.ifaw.org

Further reading

Barre, Michel, et al. *Animal Senses.*
Milwaukee: Gareth Stevens, 1998.

Day, Nancy. *Animal Experimentation:
Cruelty or Science?* Berkeley Heights, N.J.:
Enslow, 2000.

Haugen, David M., ed. *Animal
Experimentation.* Farmington Hills, Mich.:
Gale Group, 1999.

Hurley, Jennifer. *Animal Rights.* Farmington
Hills, Mich.: Gale Group. 1998.

James, Barbara. *Animal Rights.* Chicago:
Raintree, 1999.

Woods, Geraldine. *Animal Experimentation
and Testing: A Pro/Con Issue.* Berkeley
Heights, N.J.: Enslow, 1999.

Glossary

anthropomorphism giving human form or feelings to an animal or object

aquarium tanks or buildings containing water animals and plants

bill draft of a law that is presented to the legislative branch of a government and voted on

bull baiting sport in which bulldogs are pitted against restrained bulls

captive bolt electric shock given to the brain to stun an animal

cesarean section delivery of offspring by cutting into the mother's abdomen

cholera bacterial infection causing diarrhea

clone animal produced artificially from the cells of one parent. It is identical to the parent and has the same genes.

compassion feeling of pity or distress for another's suffering

coral marine animal that lives in large communities and has a stone-like skeleton

cortisones chemical hormones made in the body that carry signals through the blood to another part of the body

DNA molecule found in the cells of an organism, containing genes that have all the information needed to build and maintain the organism

domesticate keep wildlife under cultivation or as companion animals

embalmed treated with preservatives to stop decay

endangered facing extinction (dying out)

endorphins chemicals made in the body that carry a painkilling signal through the blood to another part of the body

exploitation using for one's own gain

free-range farming system where animals have more room to move around and access to the outdoors

gene length of DNA that describes one characteristic of an organism, such as eye color

genetic engineering field of science in which genes are moved or altered to make changes to organisms

genetic modification process of altering the DNA in an organism

habitat natural home of an animal or plant

hormone chemical made by the body

Hormone Replacement Therapy medical treatment for women during and after menopause

intensive farming farming for maximum production, usually highly mechanized; animals are often kept indoors

legislation laws or the process of making laws

moratorium agreed-on suspension of activity

nonintensive farming farms, such as free-range, that offer more humane conditions (but are more expensive to run) than intensive farms

nonsentient not **sentient**

neurological of the nervous system or brain

prosecution carrying out legal proceedings against someone

put down kill humanely, usually by injection

selective breeding deliberate breeding of animals to improve certain characteristics

sentience state of being sentient (*see below*)

sentient having the power of sense perception or sensation. It includes the ability to feel pain.

sheep dip chemical bath used to rid sheep of parasites. The chemicals are usually toxic.

snaring trapping animals with a wire loop that catches hold and draws in tighter

sow female adult pig

stereotypy/stereotypies repetitive movement, such as pacing, rocking, or foot chewing, performed as a reaction to stress

transgenic containing genetic material artificially moved from other organisms

vertebrate any animal with a backbone

vivisection experimentation on living animals

weaned taken off milk and started on solid food

Index